Language Brain Boosters

by
Becky Daniel

illustrated by
Nancee McClure

Cover by Nancee McClure

Copyright © Good Apple, 1992

GOOD APPLE
1204 BUCHANAN ST., BOX 299
CARTHAGE, IL 62321-0299

S I M O N & S C H U S T E R   *A Paramount Communications Company*

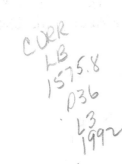

Table of Contents

GA1348

To the Teacher

Language Brain Boosters is a collection of language-based puzzles, activities and work sheets especially designed to make children think! Often many elementary language lessons involve a great deal of rote learning, and one problem facing educators is how to teach our children to think analytically. Children can often read and write words that they do not comprehend, and although memorization is an important skill, thinking skills are important, too.

To prepare your students to use the work sheets found herein, it is important to remember that reading the directions may be difficult or impossible for beginning readers. It is therefore suggested that the directions be given in small groups and the example carefully explained before children are sent back to their desks to do independent seatwork.

Language Brain Boosters includes activities to teach contractions, possessives, synonyms, homonyms, antonyms, rhyming words, metaphors, similies, abbreviations and much, much more. Other important higher thinking skills such as drawing inferences and conclusions and interpreting new ideas are also covered. The fun-filled puzzles, coloring activities, and activity sheets will make language arts an enjoyable learning experience for all.

Bonus activities are found on most pages. These activities are usually more difficult and should not be a requirement. You may choose to use the bonus activities for extra credit. Students who complete these should receive special recognition. A class competition could involve keeping track of how many bonus activities are completed by each student and rewarding those who complete a given number. Awards are found on pages 59 and 60, and a special award certificate for bonus activities is included.

GA1348

Cross One Out

Look at each row of pictures. Decide which one of the last four objects you would not need to make or do the first thing pictured in each row. Cross out the object in each row that wasn't needed.

Bonus: Draw a picture of three things you would need to build a snowman.

1

GA1348

Fun and Easy

Look at each pair of words and the pictures that follow. Color the picture in each row that is best described by both of the words.

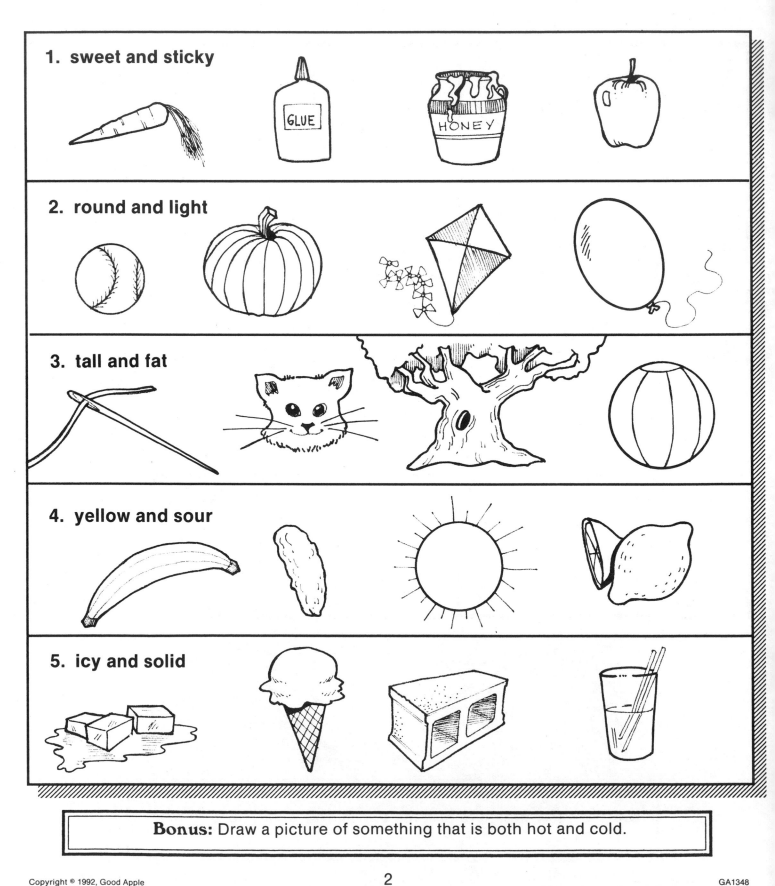

Bonus: Draw a picture of something that is both hot and cold.

GA1348

One That Is Both

Look at each pair of words and the pictures that follow. Color the picture in each row that is best described by both of the words.

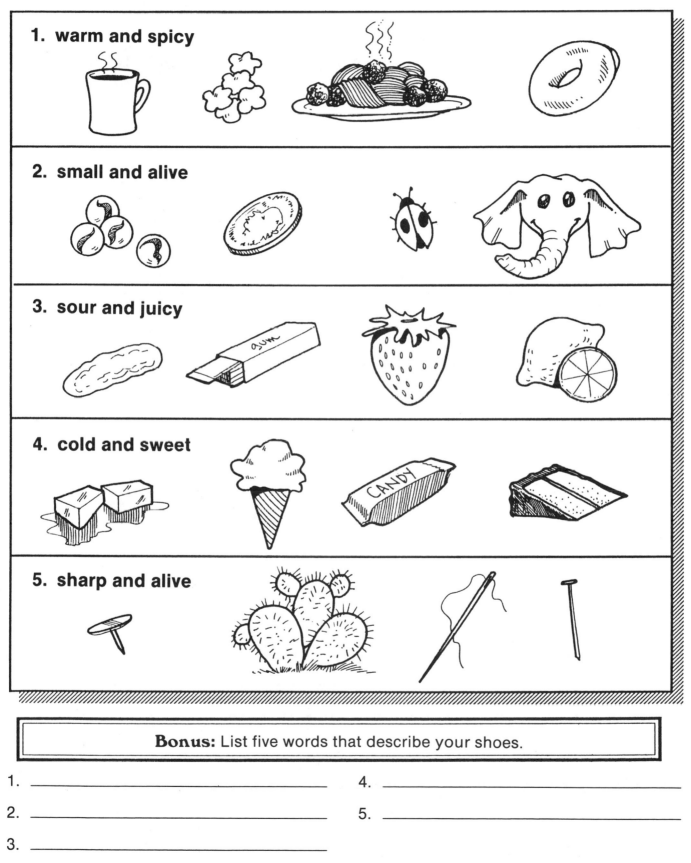

1. warm and spicy

2. small and alive

3. sour and juicy

4. cold and sweet

5. sharp and alive

Bonus: List five words that describe your shoes.

1. _____   4. _____

2. _____   5. _____

3. _____

You Decide

Read the words found in each box below. Draw something that both words describe. Example: hot chocolate is both *hot* and *sweet*. You could draw a cup of hot chocolate in the first box.

1. hot and sweet	**2. cold and sour**
3. large and alive	**4. big and soft**
5. round and red	**6. little and hard**

Bonus: Make a list of six words that describe your favorite toy.

1. _____   4. _____

2. _____   5. _____

3. _____   6. _____

GA1348

Draw Again

Read the words found in each box below. Draw something that both words describe.

1. fuzzy and green	**2. hungry and wet**
3. loud and small	**4. dangerous and not alive**
5. loud and not alive	**6. juicy and sour**

Bonus: Draw a picture of something that is not alive but loved.

GA1348

Which One?

Read the description found at the beginning of each row. Then choose the animal that is being described. Color the correct animal in each row.

Description			
1. can hop and swim	(frog)	(horse)	(elephant)
2. cannot hop or fly	(bird)	(frog)	(turtle)
3. cannot swim or fly	(bird)	(turtle)	(elephant)
4. can fly and swim	(lion)	(duck)	(elephant)
5. can fly, does not have feathers	(lion)	(duck)	(butterfly)
6. has four legs, cannot fly	(cow)	(chicken)	(butterfly)
7. is a good pet, has fur	(cat)	(cow)	(lion)

Bonus: Make a list of six words that describe your favorite animal. See if a friend can guess the animal by reading your descriptive words.

1. _____   4. _____

2. _____   5. _____

3. _____   6. _____

Picking Pets

Read the pet descriptions in each row found below. Then color the pet you think is being described.

1. a pet that can sometimes talk			
2. a pet that lives in a bowl			
3. a pet that can sing			
4. a pet you can ride			
5. a pet you can take for a walk			
6. a pet that might sleep with you			
7. a pet you cannot ride			

Bonus: List three things that describe your favorite animal.

1. _____

2. _____

3. _____

GA1348

Checking Pets

Read the list of animals. Decide if each animal can: walk, run, hop, fly, swim. Put a check mark under each word if the animal can do it. Example: A robin can walk, so put a check in the first box in the first row.

	walk	run	hop	fly	swim
1. robin					
2. hippo					
3. frog					
4. elephant					
5. duck					
6. ladybug					
7. cat					
8. horse					
9. spider					
10. child					

Bonus: Add two more animals to the list and put the check marks where needed.

GA1348

Which One?

Read and think. Then color the toy described in each row.

1. you can ride on it	(frisbee)	(skateboard)	(rag doll)
2. you can jump with it but not ride on it	(skateboard)	(tricycle)	(jump rope)
3. you cannot ride on it	(tricycle)	(rag doll)	(skateboard)
4. you can throw it	(pail and shovel)	(beach ball)	(rag doll)
5. you cannot jump on it or with it	(trampoline)	(jacks)	(jump rope)
6. you can play with it under water	(pail)	(frisbee)	(kite)
7. you can carry it	(trampoline)	(tricycle)	(pail and shovel)
8. it doesn't have wheels	(skateboard)	(tricycle)	(kite)

Bonus: Name a toy you can lift, ride and wear.

9

GA1348

Who Can See?

Read each question found below. Then decide which child or children best answer(s) the question. Write the number for the correct child or children after each question.

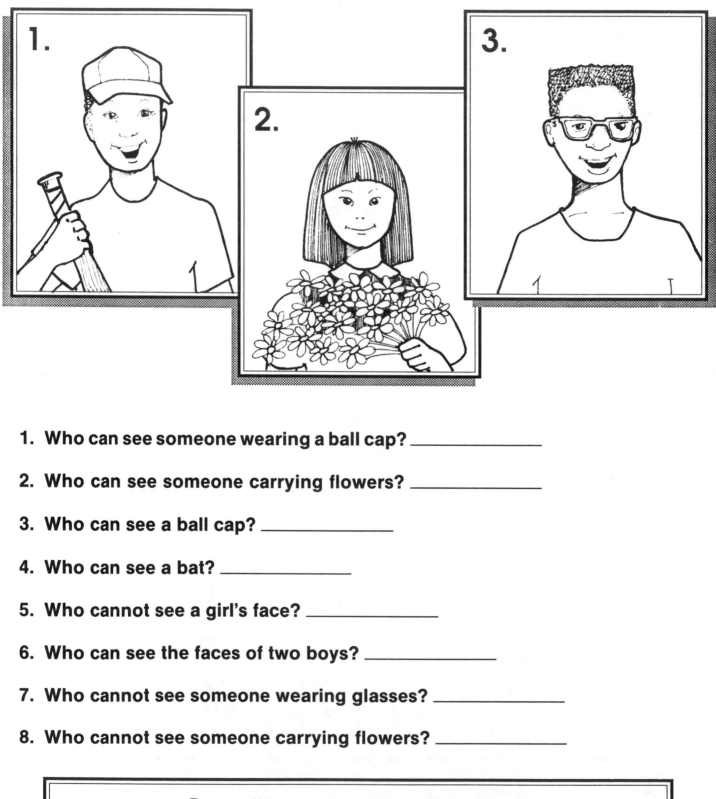

1. **Who can see someone wearing a ball cap?** _____

2. **Who can see someone carrying flowers?** _____

3. **Who can see a ball cap?** _____

4. **Who can see a bat?** _____

5. **Who cannot see a girl's face?** _____

6. **Who can see the faces of two boys?** _____

7. **Who cannot see someone wearing glasses?** _____

8. **Who cannot see someone carrying flowers?** _____

Bonus: Who can see a girl wearing glasses?

GA1348

Colorful Clowns

Read each direction found below. Think and then color the correct clown.

1. **Marvin is not sad. Color Marvin's hat *orange*.**

2. **Rita is happy, too. Color Rita's suit *yellow* with *blue* dots.**

3. **Ralph is sad. Color Ralph's hat *red*.**

4. **Color Zippo's hair *green*.**

5. **Ralph's suit is *purple*. Color Ralph's suit.**

6. **Zippo's suit is *pink*. Color it.**

7. **Finish coloring the picture any colors you choose.**

Bonus: Describe how you knew which clown was Zippo.

GA1348

Coloring Pets

Read each direction found below. Think and then color each animal.

1. **Mary's pet cannot fly or swim. Color it *orange* with *brown* stripes.**

2. **Chris' pet has *green* and *blue* feathers. Color Chris' pet.**

3. **Roger took his pet to school in a shoe box. Color Roger's pet *green*.**

4. **Max's pet is *black* with *white* spots. Color Max's pet.**

5. **Write the name of the pet owner below each animal.**

Bonus: Draw a picture of an appropriate meal for each pet.

GA1348

Weather Watch

Use the number of the picture that best answers each question found below.

1. Which day would be best for ice skating? _____

2. Which day should you wear mittens? _____

3. Which day should you take an umbrella? _____

4. Which day would be best for swimming? _____

5. Which day would you like to fly a kite? _____

6. Which day would you most like to play out doors? _____

7. Which day could be Christmas? _____

8. Which day would be best for building a snowman? _____

9. Which day is your favorite weather? _____

10. Which day would you like to go to the beach? _____

Bonus: When is your birthday? _____ Which picture is most like the weather on your birthday? _____

13

GA1348

Picture That!

Use the number of the picture that best answers each question.

1. **Which picture is happening at the zoo?** _____

2. **Which picture is happening on a warm, sunny day?** _____

3. **Which picture is of something make-believe?** _____

4. **Which picture is happening after sunset?** _____

5. **Which picture is of someone working?** _____

6. **Which picture has a flying animal?** _____

7. **Which picture is of a very cold day?** _____

8. **Which picture is of a person and his/her pet?** _____

Bonus: Draw a picture of a girl riding an imaginary animal on a warm, sunny day.

14

Measure Up!

Found in the four boxes below are objects that measure things. Use the number of each object to answer the questions.

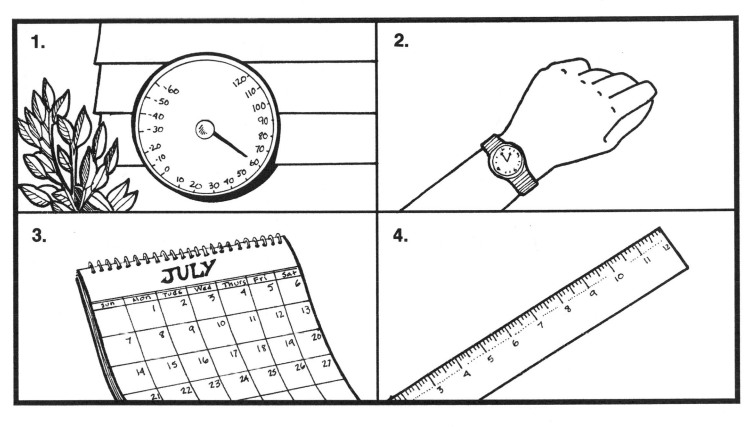

1. **Which one would you use to find out what time it is?** _____

2. **Which one would you use to measure how long your foot is?** _____

3. **Which one would you use to find out how warm it is outside?** _____

4. **Which one measures things in inches?** _____

5. **Which one measures things in minutes?** _____

6. **Which one measures things in weeks?** _____

7. **Which one measures things in degrees?** _____

8. **Which one would you use to find out what day of the week your birthday will be on?** _____

Bonus: Draw a picture of something you would use to find out if you are sick.

GA1348

Five Senses

Read and think. Then use the number or numbers of the body part that best describes how the information was received.

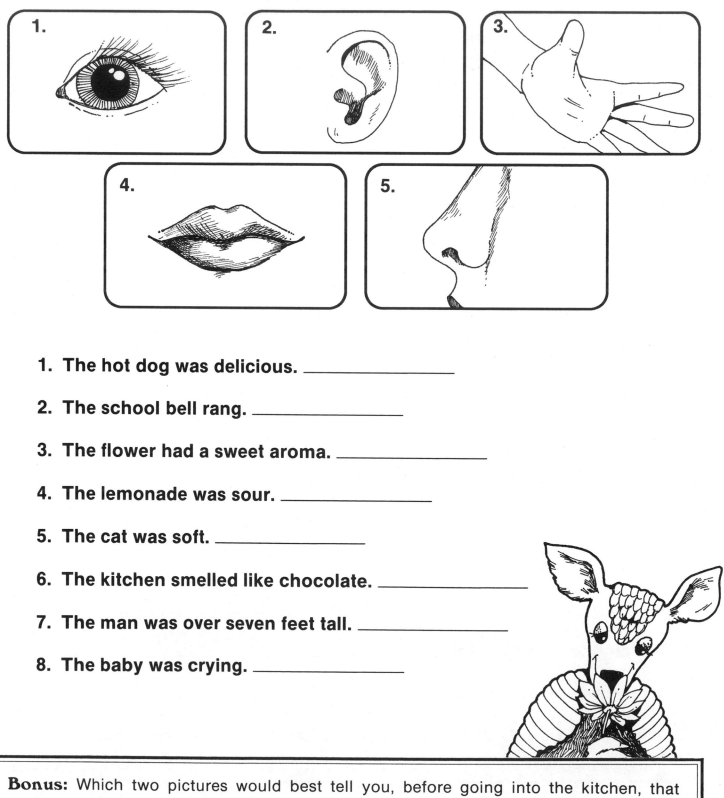

1.

2.

3.

4.

5.

1. The hot dog was delicious. _____

2. The school bell rang. _____

3. The flower had a sweet aroma. _____

4. The lemonade was sour. _____

5. The cat was soft. _____

6. The kitchen smelled like chocolate. _____

7. The man was over seven feet tall. _____

8. The baby was crying. _____

Bonus: Which two pictures would best tell you, before going into the kitchen, that someone was making popcorn?

GA1348

Drawing Compound Words

Draw a picture of a compound word for each pair of pictures found below. For Example:

(foot) + (ball) = (football)

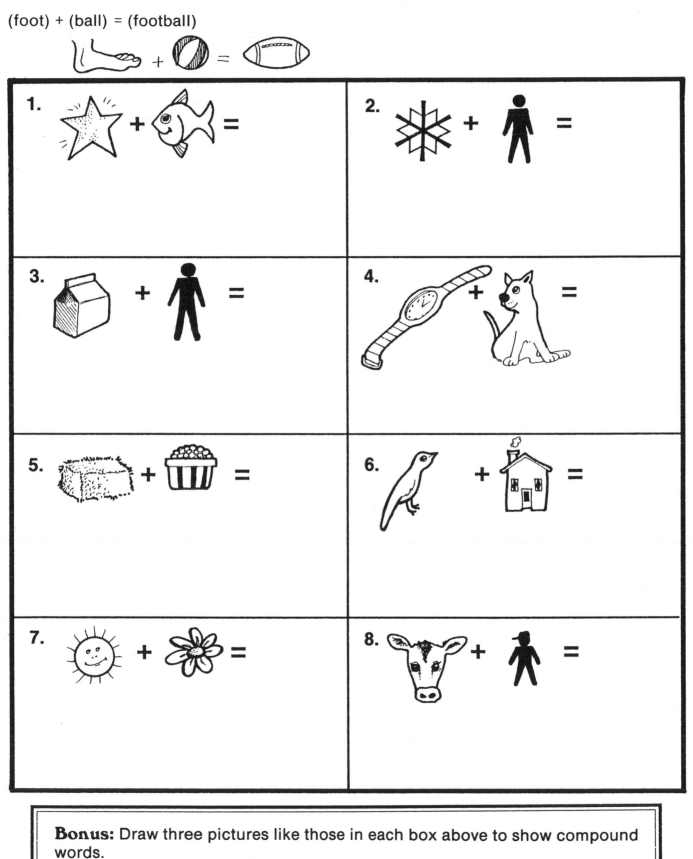

Bonus: Draw three pictures like those in each box above to show compound words.

Shhhhh, Listen

Some words have a silent letter. Say each picture word below and listen for the sound of each letter. Cross out the letters in each word that you do not hear.

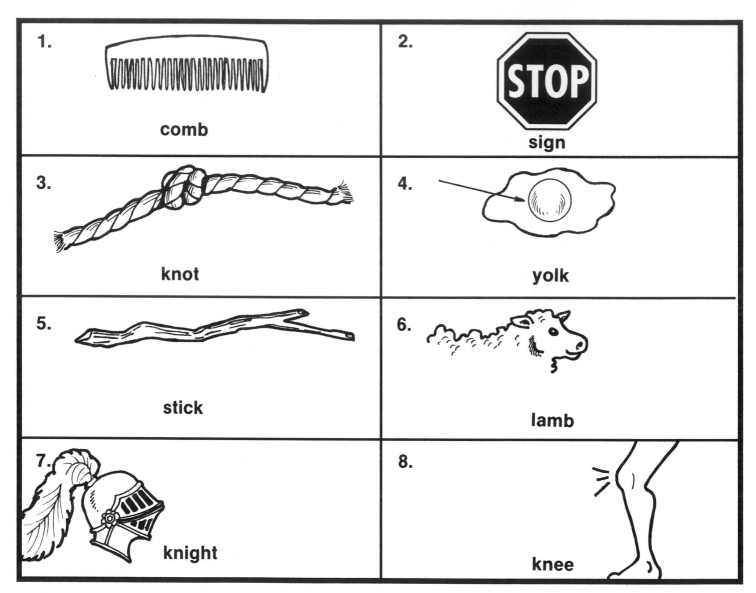

1. comb

2. sign

3. knot

4. yolk

5. stick

6. lamb

7. knight

8. knee

Bonus: Make a list of six words that have a silent letter.

1. _____   4. _____

2. _____   5. _____

3. _____   6. _____

Silent Word Pictures

Read each word with silent letters found in the boxes below. Cross out the silent letters in each word. Then draw and color a picture for each word.

1. truck	2. ghost
3. calf	4. knife
5. thumb	6. duck
7. knob	8. watch

Bonus: Draw a picture of six words that have silent letters.

GA1348

Plurals of **Y** Words

To form the plural of most words ending in the letter *y*, change the *y* to *i* and add *es*. Example: candy, candies.

1. If _____ = penny, then _____ = _____

2. If _____ = baby, then _____ = _____

3. If _____ = berry, then _____ = _____

4. If _____ = fairy, then _____ = _____

5. If _____ = canary, then _____ = _____

6. If _____ = puppy, then _____ = _____

7. If _____ = cooky, then _____ = _____

Bonus: Write the plural form for these words: donkey and monkey.

GA1348

Plurals of *S*, *Sh* or *X*

To form the plural of words ending in the letter *s*, *sh* or *x*, simply add *es* to the word. Example: brush = brushes. Write the plural form for the words, pictured in the boxes below.

1. = _____

2. = _____

3. = _____

4. = _____

5. = _____

6. = _____

Bonus: Write the plural form for the word *fish*.

GA1348

Plurals of *F* or *Fe*

To form the plural of words ending in the letter(s) *f* or *fe*, change the *f* or *fe* to *ve* and add *s*. Example: leaf = leaves. A picture has been drawn to show each word in the boxes below.

1. = _____

2. = _____

3. = _____

4. = _____

5. = _____

6. = _____

7. = _____

8. = _____

9. = _____

10. = _____

11. = _____

12. = _____

Bonus: Write the singular form for the word *dwarves*.

GA1348

Special Plural Forms

Some plural forms of words change the whole spelling of the word. Draw a line connecting the words to correct plural. The first one has been completed for you.

1. foot ——————————— men

2. ox   feet

3. man   mice

4. goose   geese

5. child   women

6. mouse   oxen

7. tooth   children

8. woman   teeth

Bonus: Write the plural form for these four words: *sheep, moose, pants, deer*.

GA1348

What Nots!

To make a *not* contraction, spell the first word and add *n't*. Example: do not = don't. Write the contraction for each word pair found below.

1. are not _____

2. were not _____

3. have not _____

4. is not _____

5. does not _____

6. could not _____

7. has not _____

8. would not _____

9. should not _____

10. did not _____

Bonus: Write a contraction using these three words: *I would have*.

GA1348

Issssss s s s

To make an *is* contraction, spell the first word and add *'s*. Example: it is = it's. Below are eight *is* contractions. Write the two words used to form each contraction.

1. **that's** _____ _____

2. **he's** _____ _____

3. **here's** _____ _____

4. **she's** _____ _____

5. **there's** _____ _____

6. **who's** _____ _____

7. **one's** _____ _____

8. **what's** _____ _____

Bonus: Add apostrophes where needed in the sentences that follow:
1. Its my cat.
2. My cat is wearing its sweater.
3. Whose house is that?
4. Whos coming with you?

Contractions

To form a *would* contraction, write the first word and add *'d*. To form an *are* contraction, write the first word and add *'re*. To form a *have* contraction, write the first word and add *'ve*. Write the two words for each contraction found below. To form an *will* contraction, write the first word and add *'ll*.

1. I've _____ _____

2. I'd _____ _____

3. You're _____ _____

4. we've _____ _____

5. they'll _____ _____

6. we're _____ _____

7. she'd _____ _____

8. we'll _____ _____

9. they're _____ _____

10. you've _____ _____

11. he'll _____ _____

12. you'll _____ _____

Bonus: Make a list of six more contractions not found above.

1. _____ 4. _____

2. _____ 5. _____

3. _____ 6. _____

GA1348

Possessives

To show that someone owns something, you use an apostrophe. Example: To describe the face of one boy, you would write, "The boy's face." If you were describing the faces of many boys you would write, "The boys' faces." Put an apostrophe in each sentence found below.

1. This is Toms house.

2. Did you see the two birds nests?

3. This is my cats bed.

4. These are the boys bikes.

5. Do you have Jills paper graded?

6. This lunch is hers.

Bonus: Place the apostrophe in the correct place in the sentences that follow:

1. This is the childrens room.
2. These are the ten mens hats.
3. This will be the girls mothers table.

Who?

A *who* word can be a person, an animal or a thing which acts. Example: a robot is a *who*. Can you find and circle *who* words in the letter maze below? Can you find ten? Fifteen?

```
A  S  T  R  O  N  A  U  T  B
U  U  O  H  A  U  N  I  E  A
N  E  M  A  N  R  T  C  A  N
T  M  A  X  N  S  D  U  C  K
B  O  X  U  E  E  D  M  H  E
A  M  O  N  K  E  Y  A  E  R
B  I  T  C  W  T  O  Y  R  R
Y  O  E  L  R  I  U  T  E  A
T  P  R  E  S  I  D  E  N  T
```

Bonus: Alphabetize the list of *who* words you circled.

GA1348

What?

A *what* word tells of an action. Examples: cried, looked, barks. Complete each sentence below by filling in the blank with an appropriate word from the *what* word bank.

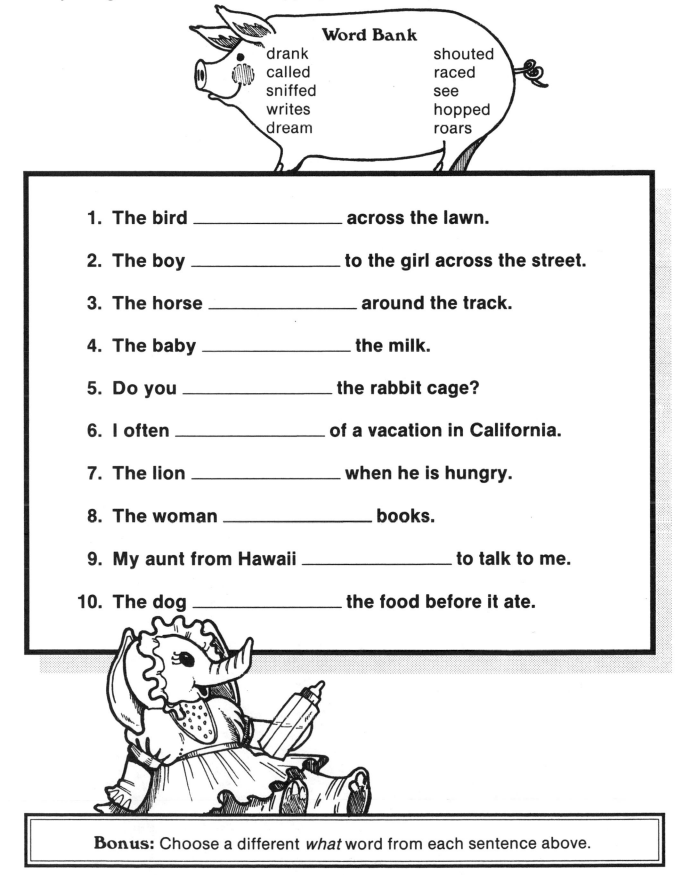

Word Bank

drank	shouted
called	raced
sniffed	see
writes	hopped
dream	roars

1. The bird _____ across the lawn.

2. The boy _____ to the girl across the street.

3. The horse _____ around the track.

4. The baby _____ the milk.

5. Do you _____ the rabbit cage?

6. I often _____ of a vacation in California.

7. The lion _____ when he is hungry.

8. The woman _____ books.

9. My aunt from Hawaii _____ to talk to me.

10. The dog _____ the food before it ate.

Bonus: Choose a different *what* word from each sentence above.

GA1348

When?

A *when* word gives a time that something happens. Example: today, at night, two weeks ago. Find and circle the *when* words found in each sentence below.

1. I cannot go to work this morning because I am ill.

2. She left for Iowa a week ago.

3. Tomorrow I will clean my room.

4. Never make a promise you cannot keep.

5. At noon we ate our sandwiches and cake.

6. At twilight we took a walk.

7. Two years ago I met a man from Tennessee.

8. You can rest whenever you feel tired.

9. I won't tell you the secret now.

10. He left early, without even saying goodbye.

Bonus: Make a new list of *when* words that could be used in each sentence above.

GA1348

Where?

A *where* word tells a place or a direction. Example: east, at the races, in the middle. Each group of *where* words found below is missing the same vowel more than once. Fill in the correct vowel in the blanks, in each *where* word. The first one has been completed for you.

1. _O_ n the m _O_ _O_ n

2. at sch ___ ___ l

3. in ___ y ___ rd

4. ___ t the d ___ iry

5. ___ nder the ch ___ rch b ___ ilding

6. b ___ hind th ___ tr ___ ___

7. on th ___ offic ___ wall

8. outs ___ de ___ ll ___ no ___ s

9. ___ n the N ___ rth P ___ le

10. n ___ ar th ___ t ___ l ___ phon ___ booth

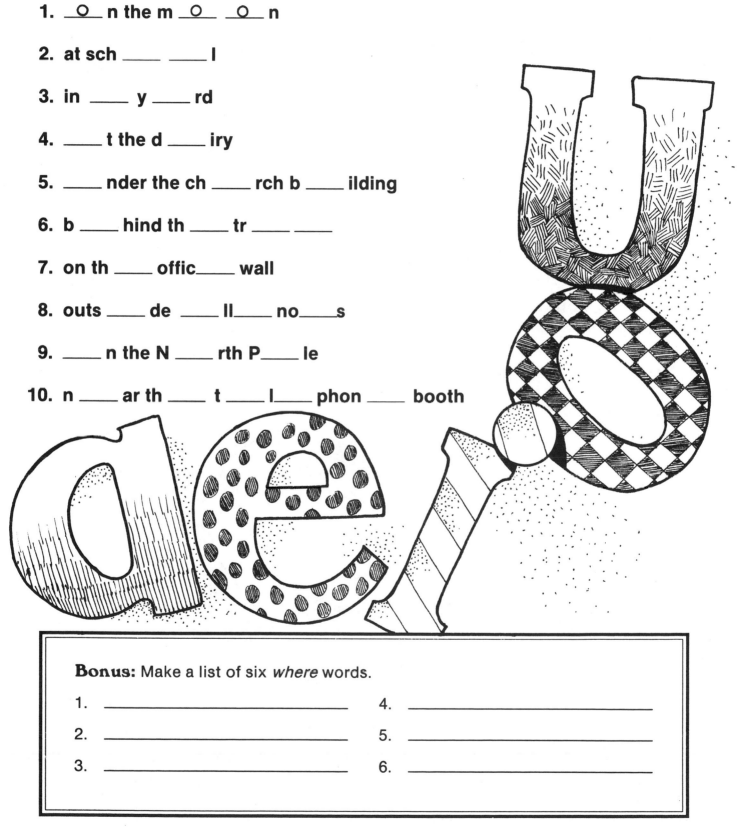

Bonus: Make a list of six *where* words.

1. _____   4. _____

2. _____   5. _____

3. _____   6. _____

GA1348

How?

A *how* word tells the manner, method or means of doing something. Examples: by cutting, with ease, quickly, without help. Draw a line connecting the correct *how* word to each sentence.

1. **How does a snail move?**

2. **How do you get from New York to California in five hours?**

3. **How do some children get to school?**

4. **How do you lift something too heavy for one person to lift?**

5. **How do you travel on water?**

6. **How do you handle a tiny bird?**

7. **How do you paste two papers together?**

8. **How do you get into the game?**

by plane

slowly

with help

gently

by school bus

by boat

with a ticket

with glue

Bonus: Write a new list of *how* for each sentence.

GA1348

Why?

A *why* word gives a reason, cause or purpose. Examples: to help, for fun, because he is tall. Underline the *why* words found in each sentence below. The first one has been completed for you.

1. I drew a picture <u>for art class.</u>

2. Amy stayed home because she was ill.

3. Eric wears glasses so he can see better.

4. Sarah went to the store to buy milk.

5. I gave Christy a rabbit because it was her birthday.

6. Richie took her to a movie because he likes her.

7. They went to Hawaii to rest.

8. Beth wore pink because she was happy.

Bonus: Make a list of six *why* words.

1. _____   4. _____

2. _____   5. _____

3. _____   6. _____

GA1348

Opposites Attract

Draw a picture in each box to show the opposites of the words listed below. The first one has been completed for you.

1. summer

2. day

3. sun

4. go

5. red

6. adult

7. valley

8. rainy

Bonus: Draw pictures of two opposite things.

GA1348

Where?

In each sentence found below there are words that tell about a place. Find the *where* words in each sentence and underline them. The first one has been completed for you.

1. He landed <u>on the moon</u>.

2. The kitten slept in my house slipper.

3. We rode our bikes to the post office.

4. They keep all the wild animals in cages.

5. Look under your bed and you'll find your shoes.

6. She vacationed in Hawaii for three weeks.

7. He keeps the reindeers at the North Pole.

8. She slipped her hand in mine.

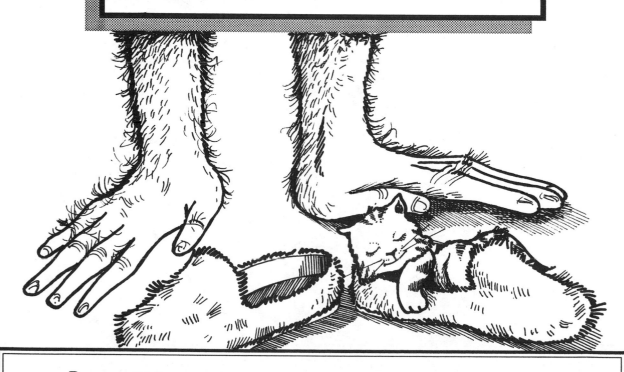

Bonus: Write a sentence and underline the words that tell where.

GA1348

Bi Is Two

Bi is a prefix that means "having two of the root words." Example: *bisect* means "to cut into two pieces." Draw a line connecting the *bi* prefix words with the appropriate definition.

1. biplane

2. biweekly

3. bicuspid

4. binoculars

5. bicycle

6. biennial

a. happening once every two years

b. a vehicle with two wheels

c. happening every two weeks

d. having two main wings

e. a tooth with two points

f. a pair of small telescopes fastened together to use with both eyes

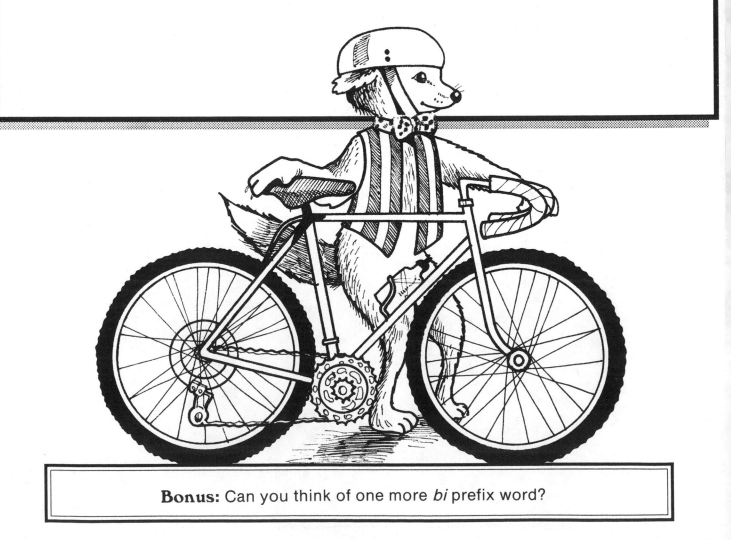

Bonus: Can you think of one more *bi* prefix word?

Multiple Meanings

Some words have more than one meaning. Example: A round toy and a dance is a *ball*. Use the clues to help you complete each multiple meaning word found below.

1. A weapon or a body part is

   a r _____

2. A creation or a skill is

   a r _____

3. To carry or an animal is a

   bea _____

4. A time or a fruit is a

   dat _____

5. To fight or a container is a

   bo _____

6. A chilly temperature or to remain calm is

   coo _____

7. To invent or a piece of money is

   coi _____

8. To pull or illustrate something is to

   dra _____

9. To give or a body part is

   han _____

10. To shake or a container is

    ja _____

11. To arrive or the ground is

    lan _____

12. To joke or a young goat is

    ki _____

GA1348

Cross One Out!

In each row of words below, one word doesn't belong. Read the words and decide how three of them are related. Then cross out the one that doesn't relate to the others in the same way. On the line under each row, list how the other three words relate to each other. The first one has been completed for you.

1. stars   galaxy   planet   ~~Sunday~~

   outer space
   _____

2. afternoon   season   second   desk
   _____

3. odd   even   grade   zero
   _____

4. smell   perfume   gold   aroma
   _____

5. sour   quiet   sweet   bitter
   _____

6. dazed   clatter   quiet   whisper
   _____

7. grapefruit   lime   date   rose
   _____

8. taffy   chocolate   popcorn   toffee
   _____

Bonus: What do these four words have in common: *walnut, palm, maple, spruce*?

38

Comparative and Superlative

A *comparative* is the form of a word that compares two things. Examples: smaller, taller, greener. A *superlative* is the form of a word that compares more than two things. Examples: smallest, tallest, greenest. Complete the comparative and superlative word chart found below. The first one has been completed for you.

1. big	bigger	biggest
2. white		
3. soft		
4. clean		
5. slow		
6. poor		
7. long		
8. safe		
9. sad		
10. cold		

Bonus: Write the comparative and superlative form for the word *good*.

GA1348

Comparing

In each sentence found below, write the comparative or superlative form of each word given in parenthesis. Remember: *er* compares two objects and *est* compares more than two.

1. That pig is the (fat) _____ of the whole litter.

2. This page of math is (easy) _____ than yesterday's page.

3. That man is the (rich) _____ man in the country.

4. My foot is (long) _____ than your foot.

5. I won an award for having the (clean) _____ desk in our class.

6. That is the (sad) _____ story I've ever heard.

7. Monday was the (cold) _____ day of the week.

8. My cat is (soft) _____ than my dog.

Bonus: Write the comparative and superlative forms for the word *bad*.

_____   _____

GA1348

Homonyms

Homonyms are words that are pronounced the same but spelled differently. Examples: *sun* and *son* or *male* and *mail*. Find and circle the homonym for each word found in the word bank.

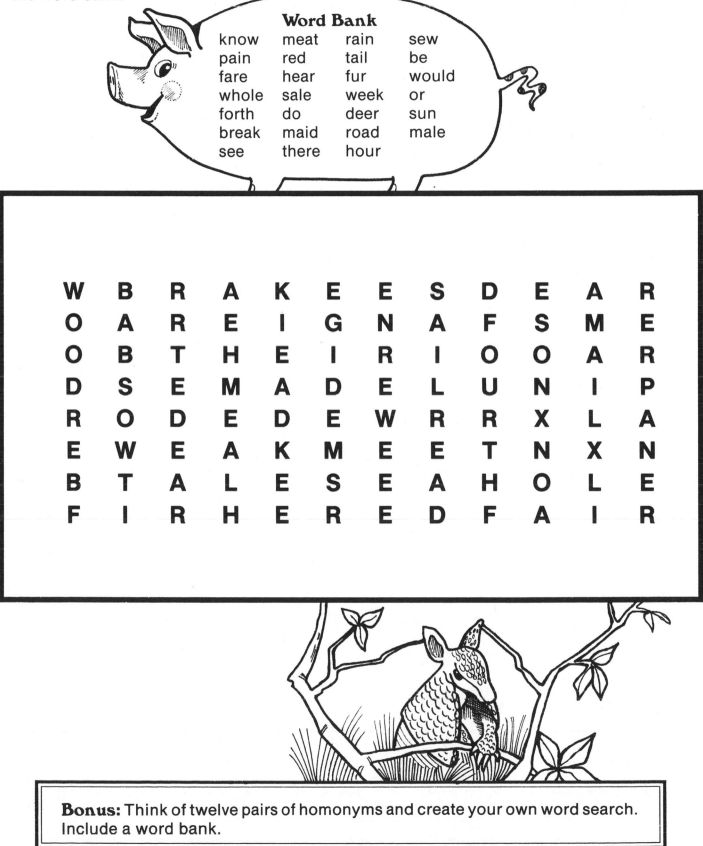

Word Bank

know	meat	rain	sew
pain	red	tail	be
fare	hear	fur	would
whole	sale	week	or
forth	do	deer	sun
break	maid	road	male
see	there	hour	

```
W  B  R  A  K  E  E  S  D  E  A  R
O  A  R  E  I  G  N  A  F  S  M  E  R
O  B  T  H  E  I  R  I  O  O  A  R
D  S  E  M  A  D  E  L  U  N  I  P
R  O  D  E  D  E  W  R  R  X  L  A  N  E
E  W  E  A  K  M  E  E  T  N  X  R
B  T  A  L  E  S  E  A  H  O  L  E
F  I  R  H  E  R  E  D  F  A  I  R
```

Bonus: Think of twelve pairs of homonyms and create your own word search. Include a word bank.

GA1348

More Homonyms

In the story found below, homonyms have been used incorrectly. Cross out each incorrectly used homonym and write the correct word above it. Use the homonym word bank to help you.

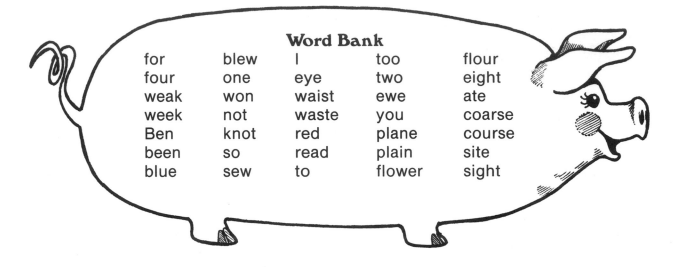

Word Bank

for	blew	I	too	flour
four	one	eye	two	eight
weak	won	waist	ewe	ate
week	not	waste	you	coarse
Ben	knot	red	plane	course
been	so	read	plain	site
blue	sew	to	flower	sight

Four to weaks eye

have Ben baking cakes

with read icing. Ewe

can knot waist flower

and sugar, sew eye

eight every won of the

cakes. Of coarse, my

waist is getting bigger;

Eye look like a site.

The plane fact is, I blue

my diet.

Bonus: Write a sentence that contains two pairs of homonyms.

GA1348

Synonyms

Synonyms are words that mean the same thing. Examples: absent, away; conduct, behave; afraid, fearful. Unscramble the words in the right column to spell synonyms for the words in the left column. The first one has been completed for you.

1. evil   dab   bad

2. begin   rastt   _____

3. large   gib   _____

4. close   rena   _____

5. desire   hswi   _____

6. enjoy   ekli   _____

7. present   fgit   _____

8. giant   ghue   _____

9. ill   ksic   _____

10. little   lasml   _____

11. price   tsco   _____

12. real   etru   _____

Bonus: Unscramble these letters to spell two synonyms for the answer to an addition problem.

m t t s o u a l

43

GA1348

Connecting Synonyms

Draw a line to connect the synonyms. The first one has been completed for you.

1. quiz	teach
2. warrior	plot
3. train	story
4. tale	form
5. sum	soldier
6. town	robber
7. thief	total
8. shout	city
9. shape	test
10. rear	yell
11. plan	strange
12. odd	back

Bonus: Make a list of six synonym pairs that describe you.

Antonyms

Antonyms are words that are opposites. Examples; black, white; work, play. Draw a picture in each box found below to show the antonym for the word listed. The first one has been completed for you.

cold	old	front
little	happy	empty
clean	day	queen

Bonus: Draw a picture of a pair of antonyms.

GA1348

More Antonyms

In each sentence found below, there is an incorrectly used antonym. If you replace the word with a correct antonym, the sentence will make sense. There are many correct answers. The first one has been completed for you.

                 old

1. The car was so new, it was falling apart.

2. She hid over the bed so no one would see her.

3. The elephant was so little it took hours to wash it.

4. It is very quiet in the city because there are millions of people.

5. I got an A because I spelled all the words incorrectly.

6. The basket was heavy because it was empty.

7. My little sister is two years older than I.

8. We go to bed at eight o'clock each morning.

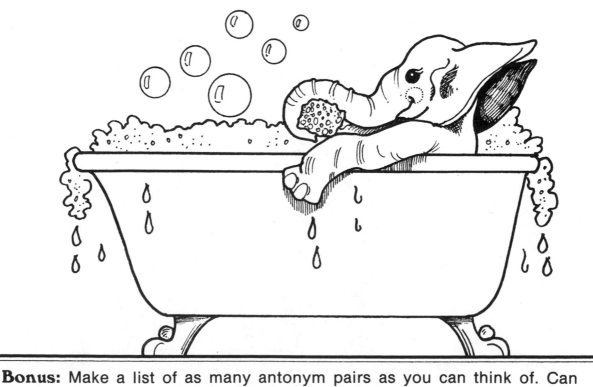

Bonus: Make a list of as many antonym pairs as you can think of. Can you list ten pairs? Twelve? Twenty?

Rhyming Words

Rhyming words end with the same sound. Examples: cab, dab, jab and crab. Draw a picture of a word that rhymes with each word found in the boxes below.

black	tag	page
mail	cane	bake
jam	plan	hand
ban	cape	lap

Bonus: Draw an animal and a flower that rhyme with *Bill*.

GA1348

More Rhyming Words

Use a pair of rhyming words to complete each sentence found below. The first one has been completed for you.

1. The clouds grew _____dark_____ in the _____park_____ so we took our picnic and went home before it started to rain.

2. I heard a _____ of thunder and saw a _____ of lightning, then it started to rain.

3. We rolled the big _____ down the _____ of the school.

4. At _____ we went outside our cabin and saw a _____ on the front lawn.

5. My grandfather said we could _____ on the _____ piled high in the barn.

6. We sat on the _____ and ate a _____ while we listened to the ocean waves pounding on the sand.

7. You could hear the whole _____ _____ when we won the last basketball game of the season.

8. I like to ride my _____ _____ down hills in the snow.

Bonus: Write a sentence with two or more rhyming words in it.

GA1348

Metaphors

A metaphor is the use of a word or phrase in a way that is different from its usual use. Metaphors are used to show a likeness to something. Example: A curtain of darkness fell over the city. The darkness was *like* a curtain but it wasn't really a curtain. See if you can guess the metaphors for each picture shown in the boxes below. Write each one on the blank found in the box.

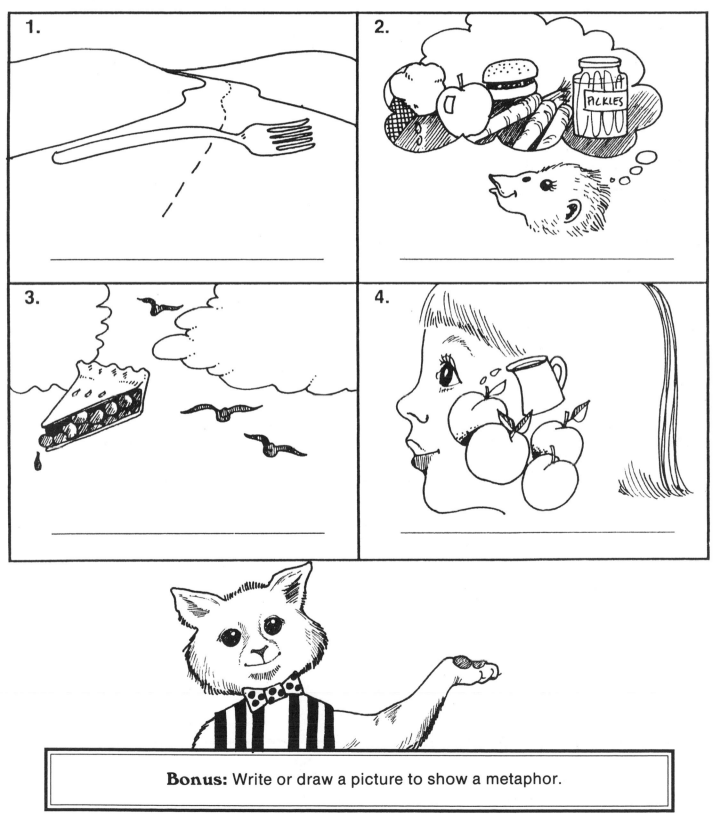

1. _____

2. _____

3. _____

4. _____

Bonus: Write or draw a picture to show a metaphor.

49

GA1348

Similes

A simile is a figure of speech in which two things that are different in most ways are said to be alike by using either the word *as* or *like*. Example: She's as sweet as candy. Draw a cartoon picture to show each simile listed in the boxes found below.

1.

She sings like a bird.

2.

He's as thin as a rail.

3.

The horse runs like lightning.

4.

She walks like a snail.

5.

Her hair is white as snow.

6.

He's sharp as a tack.

Bonus: Write or draw a cartoon to show a simile.

GA1348

Abbreviations

An abbreviation is a shortened form of a word or phrase. Look up the following abbreviations in a dictionary. Write the whole word or phrase for each one.

1. **a.m.** _____

2. **lat.** _____

3. **hvy.** _____

4. **pkg.** _____

5. **CA** _____

6. **secy.** _____

7. **Wed.** _____

8. **Feb.** _____

Bonus: Make up an abbreviation for your first, middle and last names.

GA1348

Dictionary Dig

A dictionary tells many things about a word. Besides telling the meaning(s) of a word, it also shows how to pronounce the word. Look up each word found below and write the pronunciation as it appears in your dictionary. Include each syllable separated by a dot.

1. **hungry** _____

2. **afternoon** _____

3. **government** _____

4. **hamsters** _____

5. **traffic** _____

6. **mountain** _____

7. **graduate** _____

8. **audience** _____

Bonus: Alphabetize the list of words found above.

1. _____   5. _____

2. _____   6. _____

3. _____   7. _____

4. _____   8. _____

GA1348

Two-Way Words

Some words have more than one correct spelling. Look up the words listed below and next to each one, write the variant spelling.

1. lovable _____

2. ax _____

3. orangutan _____

4. savior _____

5. gasoline _____

6. fiber _____

7. marvelous _____

8. gray _____

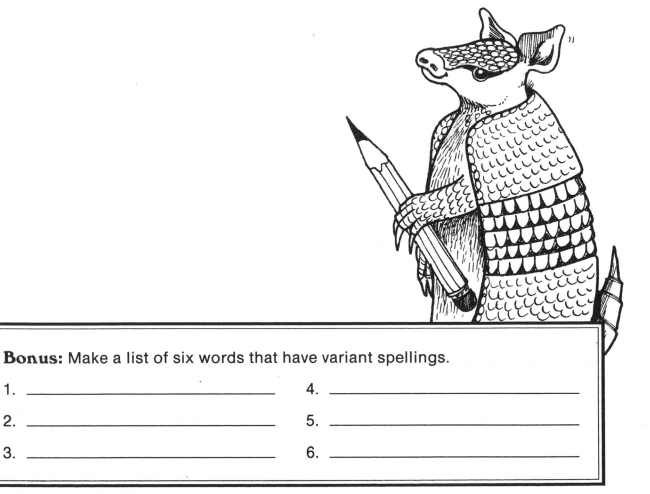

Bonus: Make a list of six words that have variant spellings.

1. _____ 4. _____

2. _____ 5. _____

3. _____ 6. _____

GA1348

Guide Words

On each page of the dictionary, two guide words are found at the top of the page. The guide words are the first and last words found on that page of the dictionary. Look at the guide words found below. Then decide if each of the words found below would or would not be found on that page in the dictionary. The first one has been completed for you.

A.

twinkle   **urban**

1. type
2. up
3. twinge
4. tug

1. yes
2. yes
3. no
4. no

B.

knob

1. lame
3. lie

launch

2. lake
4. knock

C.

pack

1. package
3. pad

parcel

2. pacific
4. patch

Bonus: Write two guide words that could appear on the page with these words: jiggle, jigsaw; irony, jot

Answer Key

Cross One Out page 1
1. ice cream
2. ice cream cone
3. garden hose
4. carrot

Fun and Easy page 2
Answers may vary.
1. honey
2. balloon
3. tree
4. lemon
5. ice cubes
Bonus: Answers may vary, could be a hot fudge sundae.

One That Is Both page 3
1. spaghetti
2. beetle
3. lemon
4. ice cream cone
5. cactus

You Decide page 4
Answers may vary.

Draw Again page 5
Answers may vary.

Which One? page 6
1. frog
2. turtle
3. pig
4. duck
5. butterfly
6. cow
7. cat

Picking Pets page 7
1. parrot
2. fish
3. bird
4. horse
5. dog
6. cat
7. bird

Checking Pets page 8

	walk	run	hop	fly	swim
robin	X	X	X	X	
hippo	X	X			X
frog			X		X
elephant	X	X			X
duck	X	X		X	X
ladybug	X	X		X	
cat	X	X			X
horse	X	X			X
spider	X	X	X		
child	X	X	X		X

Which One? page 9
1. skateboard
2. jump rope
3. doll
4. ball
5. jacks
6. goggles and snorkel
7. sand pail
8. kite

Who Can See? page 10
1. 2,3
2. 1,3
3. 1, 2, 3
4. 1, 2, 3
5. 2
6. 2
7. 3
8. 2
Bonus: No one

Colorful Clowns page 11
1. Marvin is clown #2, his hat is orange.
2. Rita is clown #4, her suit is yellow with blue dots.
3. Ralph is clown #3, his hat is red.
4. Clown #1 is Zippo, his hair is green.
5. #3 clown's suit is purple.
6. #1 clown's suit is pink.

Coloring Pets page 12
1. Mary's pet is the cat, it is orange with brown stripes.
2. Parrot has green and blue feathers.
3. Frog is green.
4. Dog is black with white spots.
5. Mary, cat; Chris, parrot; Roger, frog; Max, dog

Weather Watch page 13
1. 2
2. 2,4
3. 1
4. 3
5. 3
6. will vary
7. will vary
8. 4
9. will vary
10. 3

Picture That! page 14
1. 1
2. 2
3. 3
4. 3
5. 1
6. 3
7. 1
8. 2

Measure Up! page 15
1. 2
2. 4
3. 1
4. 4
5. 2
6. 3
7. 1
8. 3
Bonus: Thermometer

Five Senses page 16
1. 4
2. 2
3. 5
4. 4
5. 3
6. 5
7. 1
8. 2
Bonus: 2 and 5

GA1348

Drawing Compound Words page 17
1. starfish
2. snowman
3. milkman
4. watchdog
5. strawberry
6. birdhouse
7. sunflower
8. cowboy

Shhhhhh, Listen page 18
1. b 5. c
2. g 6. b
3. k 7. k
4. l 8. k

Silent Word Pictures page 19
1. c 5. b
2. h 6. c
3. l 7. k
4. k 8. t

Plurals of *Y* Words page 20
1. pennies
2. babies
3. berries
4. fairies
5. canaries
6. puppies
7. cookies
Bonus: donkeys, monkeys

Plurals of *S, Sh* or *X* page 21
1. buses
2. dishes
3. boxes
4. churches
5. crosses
6. foxes
Bonus: fish or fishes

Plurals of *F* or *Fe* page 22
1. knife 7. calf
2. calves 8. thieves
3. wolf 9. thief
4. loaves 10. knives
5. loaf 11. elf
6. wolves 12. elves
Bonus: Dwarf

Special Plural Forms page 23
1. foot, feet
2. ox, oxen
3. man, men
4. goose, geese
5. child, children
6. mouse, mice
7. tooth, teeth
8. woman, women
Bonus: Words do not change with plural form.

What Nots! page 24
1. aren't 6. couldn't
2. weren't 7. hasn't
3. haven't 8. wouldn't
4. isn't 9. shouldn't
5. doesn't 10. didn't
Bonus: I'd have

Issssss s s s page 25
1. that is
2. he is
3. here is
4. she is
5. there is
6. who is
7. one is
8. what is
Bonus: 1. It's my cat.
2. My cat is wearing its sweater.
3. Whose house is that?
4. Who's coming with you?

Contractions page 26
1. I have 7. she would
2. I would 8. we will
3. you are 9. they are
4. we have 10. you have
5. they will 11. he will
6. we are 12. you will

Possessives page 27
1. Tom's
2. birds'
3. cat's
4. boys'
5. Jill's
6. hers
Bonus: 1. children's
2. men's
3. girls' mother's or girl's mother's

Who? page 28

Bonus: Ann   Ed   rat
ant   man   Sue
astronaut   Max   teacher
aunt   May   Tom
baby   mom   toy
banker   monkey   uncle
box   nurse   you
duck   president

GA1348

What? page 29

1. hopped
2. shouted
3. raced
4. drank
5. see
6. dream
7. roars
8. writes
9. called
10. sniffed

When? page 30

1. this morning
2. a week ago
3. Tomorrow
4. Never
5. At noon
6. At twilight
7. Two years ago
8. whenever
9. now
10. early
Bonus: Once upon a time

Where? page 31

1. on the moon
2. at school
3. in a yard
4. at the dairy
5. under the church building
6. behind the tree
7. on the office wall
8. outside Illinois
9. on the North Pole
10. near the telephone booth

How? page 32

1. slowly
2. by plane
3. by school bus
4. with help
5. by boat
6. gently
7. with glue
8. with a ticket

Why? page 33

1. for art class
2. because she was ill
3. so he can see better
4. to buy milk
5. because it was her birthday
6. because he likes her
7. to rest
8. because she was happy

Opposites Attract page 34

1. winter
2. night
3. moon
4. stop
5. green
6. baby
7. mountain
8. sunny

Where? page 35

1. on the moon
2. in my house slipper
3. to the post office
4. in cages
5. under your bed
6. in Hawaii
7. at the North Pole
8. in mine

Bi Is Two page 36

1. d
2. c
3. e
4. f
5. b
6. a

Multiple Meanings page 37

1. arm
2. art
3. bear
4. date
5. box
6. cool
7. coin
8. draw
9. hand
10. jar
11. land
12. kid

Cross One Out! page 38

1. Sunday (outer space)
2. desk (time)
3. grade (numbers)
4. gold (odor)
5. quiet (taste)
6. dazed (sound)
7. rose (foods)
8. popcorn (candy)
Bonus: trees

Comparative and Superlative page 39

1. bigger, biggest
2. whiter, whitest
3. softer, softest
4. cleaner, cleanest
5. slower, slowest
6. poorer, poorest
7. longer, longest
8. safer, safest
9. sadder, saddest
10. colder, coldest
Bonus: better, best

Comparing page 40

1. fattest
2. easier
3. richest
4. longer
5. cleanest
6. saddest
7. coldest
8. softer
Bonus: worse, worst

GA1348

Homonyms page 41

More Homonyms page 42

For two weeks I have been baking cakes with red icing. You cannot waste flour and sugar, so I ate every one of the cakes. Of course, my waist is getting bigger; I look like a sight! The plain fact is, I blew my diet.

Synonyms page 43

1. bad
2. start
3. big
4. near
5. wish
6. like
7. gift
8. huge
9. sick
10. small
11. cost
12. true

Bonus: sum, total

Connecting Synonyms page 44

1. quiz, test
2. warrior, soldier
3. train, teach
4. tale, story
5. sum, total
6. town, city
7. thief, robber
8. shout, yell
9. shape, form
10. rear, back
11. plan, plot
12. odd, strange

Antonyms page 45

1. hot
2. young or new
3. back
4. big
5. sad
6. full
7. dirty
8. night
9. king

More Antonyms page 46

1. The car was so old, it was falling apart.
2. She hid under the bed so no one would see her.
3. The elephant was so big it took hours to wash it.
4. It is very noisy in the city because there are millions of people.
5. I got an A because I spelled all the words correctly.
6. The basket was light because it was empty. Or, the basket was heavy because it was full.
7. My little sister is two years younger than I. Or, my big sister is two years older than I.
8. We go to bed at eight o'clock each night.

Rhyming Words page 47
Pictures may vary.

1. black: sack
2. tag: bag, flag
3. page: cage
4. mail: snail
5. cane: plane, pane
6. bake: cake, lake, snake
7. jam: ham, clam, ram, lamb
8. plan: can, man, tan
9. hand: band, sand
10. ban: can, fan, man
11. cape: grape, tape
12. lap: cap, map

Bonus: whippoorwill, daffodil

More Rhyming Words page 48
Answers may vary.

1. dark, park
2. clash, flash
3. ball, hall
4. dawn, fawn
5. play, hay
6. beach, peach
7. team, scream
8. red, sled

Metaphors page 49

1. fork in the road
2. food for thought
3. pie in the sky
4. peaches and cream complexion

Similes page 50
Pictures may vary.

Abbreviations page 51

1. ante meridiem
2. latitude
3. heavy
4. package
5. California
6. secretary
7. Wednesday
8. February

Dictionary Dig page 52
Dictionaries may vary.

1. hun' gry
2. af'ter noon
3. guv'ern ment
4. ham' sters
5. traf' ik
6. moun' tin
7. grad' u ate
8. o' di ens

Two-Way Words page 53

1. loveable
2. axe
3. oranghutan
4. saviour
5. gasolene
6. fibre
7. marvellous
8. grey

Guide Words page 54

A. 1. yes
   2. yes
   3. no
   4. no

B. 1. yes
   2. yes
   3. no
   4. yes

C. 1. yes
   2. no
   3. yes
   4. no

Bonus: Answers may vary.

GA1348

Language Certificate of Award

For _____

_____   _____
Date   **Signature**

Plurals and Contractions Award

To _____

_____

Antonym, Synonym and Homonym Award!

GOOD JOB!

To _____

_____

59
GA1348

★ BONUS ★
AWARD
CERTIFICATE

For _____

_____   _____
Date   Signature

FANTASTIC JOB!

To _____

Keep Up
The
Good Work
In
Language!!

To _____

GA1348